Since Corona Ruined Our Trip to the Library...

poems by

Beth Gulley

Finishing Line Press
Georgetown, Kentucky

Since Corona Ruined Our Trip to the Library…

Copyright © 2022 by Beth Gulley
ISBN 978-1-64662-995-4 First Edition
All rights reserved under International and Pan-American Copyright Conventions. No part of this book may be reproduced in any manner whatsoever without written permission from the publisher, except in the case of brief quotations embodied in critical articles and reviews.

ACKNOWLEDGMENTS

"The Harpist" first appeared in *Thorny Locust*
"Trees" and "Investing" first appeared in *Kansas English*

Publisher: Leah Huete de Maines
Editor: Christen Kincaid
Cover Art: Beth Gulley
Author Photo: Susan McSpadden
Cover Design: Elizabeth Maines McCleavy

Order online: www.finishinglinepress.com
also available on amazon.com

Author inquiries and mail orders:
Finishing Line Press
PO Box 1626
Georgetown, Kentucky 40324
USA

Table of Contents

Glisten 1

Beginner's Curiosity 2

Hope Still Bubbles 3

Investing 4

Cat VS Hummingbird 5

Trees 6

One Woman Can 7

List of Delights 8

Apophis 9

Almost Everything Could Be Shorter 10

Now We Have Your Card on Fire 11

Support Chocolate 12

A Good Tidy Well-Played Game 13

A Fox Flickers 14

We Quit 15

You Have Been Chosen 16

Strike Two 17

Really 18

The Harpist 19

Jose and I 20

For Jeremy, Israel, and Asher

Glisten

Do-good-ers
hike the bridal trail
armed with trash bags.
Like Pizzaro
they stumble
on the glistening city.
In this case
the glisten shines
from broken glass
and rusted cans.
They rush to fill their bags,
hoping to restore
the eye sore
to pristine forest.
They dig deep enough
to find rusted bed springs
and moonshine bottles
and a carpet of moss
overgrowing more glass.
Like Pizzaro,
they realize
this is vaster
and older than
they first thought.
Unlike Pizzaro,
they go home
and leave it
for another day.

Beginner's Curiosity

The batik
broke rules.
Not expertly
but by beginners
curiosity.
The only wax
covered the center
where lovers
in a boat
were stenciled in.
The fabric
dyed blue
was later sprinkled
at the top
to look like
the denouement
of a firework show.
Then off to the sink.
All the wax melted
under hot water.
The batik dried
into something worth saving.
And the art teacher
never knew who
clogged the sink.

Hope Still Bubbles

Out my window
the pear tree
still flowers
despite
freezing rain
and hail.

In my room
hope still bubbles
despite
stay at home
orders
and fear
of getting sick.

Here's hoping
the tree and I
make it to summer
and forget
the strain
that brought
us there.

Investing

I am a consumer
buying coffee from Tyler
on my morning walk.
After my run
I buy snacks
from Crystal
at the gas station.
I keep the online
thrift and bookstores
hopping,
and I buy stamps
from the US
Postal Service.

I am a task master
making writing students
list fifty things
to do before they die,
then write down
the steps to make
one of these
hopes come true.
I won't let them
off the hook.

I am building
something
with the power
of my dollar
and the force
of my will.
I am making
little investments
in the future
I hope to have.

Cat VS Hummingbird

Cat can do this
better than me.
She naps, eats,
watches squirrels,
claws the couch.
She likes the
extra laps to
curl up in
now we all
work from home.
I have no feline
in me. I'm a hummingbird.
I move quickly.
I migrate the longest
of any bird.
Let's hope
in hummingbird fashion
I can also
go into torpor
to survive
the forced
isolation.

Trees

Back in sixth grade I learned
Trees are the Kindest Thing I Know
for Friday afternoon recitation
at Aunt Hazel's tiny Christian school
where twenty students sat in what
should have been a living room.

Little did I know what I was saying.
It just rolled like a chocolate drop
on my tongue.

Now after all the climate science
and well-being research,
I learn trees can capture carbon,
prevent erosion, cool the planet,
lower our heart rates,
reduce stress hormone production,
and improve creativity
all without lifting a finger.

I realize trees really are
the kindest things I know.

One Woman Can
    (A found poem from the Mary Kay Look Book)

The look
of women
on tested pages
reveal
five-minute
younger looking skin
and waterproof lines.

I think,
just for spring,
clear the way.
Be uncomplicated.
Drop the faux glow.
Explore,
Unearth,
Light up,
Natural, inspired beauty.

List of Delights

This American Life on the radio
Free coffee at the gas station
Automatic car washes
Twenty dollars in the pocket
of some forgotten jeans
Passing my dream house
Hanging out with my sons
The joy in your eyes
when I walk in the room
Even in this wobbly world
wonders still abound.

Apophis

A giant asteroid was predicted
to hit earth on your
sixty sixth birthday
(a Friday the 13th).
But in 2013 it swung
near enough to measure
and the apocalypse
we feared was avoided.
In fact, future asteroids
may be avoided by gentle
pushes like paper to a hand.
Much like a soft answer
or a joke can turn a room.
Your birthday will still be sweet
without the explosion.

Almost Everything Could Be Shorter

Almost everything
in life could be shorter.
In particular, both George Orwell
and Donald Murray's
essays advocating concision
could both be cut in half.

But the boat ride with you
across Lake Victoria
during which a baby hippo
swam away from his mother
and flamingos landed
on a nearby log
could have lasted forever.

Now We Have Your Card on Fire

Now that we have
your card on fire
you can order
whatever you want
from the bar
as long as the sparks
from your card
don't incinerate
the rest of the hotel.

Support Chocolate

I find
coffee and support chocolate
to take on my flight.
I dig through my purse
for the documentation,
but the flight security
waves me through.
No one needs proof
for support chocolate.

A Good Tidy Well-Played Game

A good tidy well-played game.
Each player knows their role.
The goal is clear.
The squirrel climbs the balcony,
knocks over the bird feeder,
and the sparrows clean up
from the ground, leaving just enough
for the ants to carry off,
and the remainder
fall into the flowerpot
and turn up as volunteer sunflowers.
It's been a good season.

A Fox Flickers

A fox
flickers
in a field
flanked by
a factory
and a freeway.

Too wild, too quick.
I snap his photo
but it doesn't stick.

Like most
empty fields
these days.
Just a flash
and a memory.

We Quit

You make language really hard.
You lock us into either/or all or nothing.
You cut out all the first person collective and leave us with ugly
    tweets.
We quit. We are going back to drums
and smoke signals.

You Have Been Chosen

You have been chosen
for a special price
on plus size dresses
and nineteen-dollar
plane tickets
to half of somewhere
you don't want to go.

Some of the time
Google reads your mind
so well you think about
getting a tin foil hat
and ads for Reynolds wrap
pop up in you feed.

But other times
you wonder
just exactly what
does Google know
about your future
that you will need
a fat dress and
a one-way ticket
to Garden City.

Strike Two

Strike two.
Your extra
chances
wear thin.

For some
the baseball
metaphor
is too generous
to represent
reality.

For others
life is a game
of t-ball
with our dad.
We get
unlimited chances
to hit the ball.

But those
whose big win
was getting
out of bed
and walking
on the diamond,
strike two
means you're
in the game.

Way to go!

Really

The artichoke
is really
an edible version
of the thistle.
When cooked
it might discolor
due to enzymatic browning
and chlorophyll oxidation.
A little vinegar prevents
discoloration.

Motherhood
is really
something that happens
when you have a baby.
There is no guarantee
that your mother
won't leave you
alone in your infant seat
on the lake shore
while she swims
or talks on the phone.
No amount of vinegar
can prevent this.

The Harpist

I remember tonight's performer
as a college student.
He sprawled across the desk
with his black boots
kicked out into the aisle.
He wrote brilliantly
but never turned in
finished products.

I don't introduce myself
after the beautiful
harp performance.
People should be allowed
to live in the present—
not be ambushed by
their former selves.

Like my cat—
once a stray
who rode thirty miles
on the motor
of a towed car—
is now the belle
of our home—
the harpist
is no longer a student,
but the darling
everyone in this crowded room
has paid to mesmerize
us with his music.

Jose and I

Jose and I
chat about cheese
in an interfaith
art zone
I'd not been to before.
The GPS led me here,
but I didn't believe it
and parked in the dark
two blocks away.
What a relief
to come into the light
and find a familiar face.

Beth **Gulley** lives in Spring Hill, Kansas and teaches writing at Johnson County Community College. She has an MA from UMKC and a PhD from the University of Kansas. When not writing about teaching, Beth primarily writes poetry.

She in 2018 published a chapbook, *$!*# Hole Countries: A Find and Replace Meditation.* Her poems also appear in the *Bards Against Hunger Anthology, From Everywhere a Little: A Migration Anthology,* the *Thorny Locust,* and *The Gasconade Review Presents: Storm A'Comin', Kansas Letters to a Young Poet,* and the *105 Meadowlark Reader.* She has been a proud member of the Facebook group 365 Poems in 365 Days since 2015, and her poems appear in all three of the 365 Poems in 365 Days anthologies.

Beth serves on the Riverfront Reading Committee and is a Writer's Place board member. She loves thrift store shopping, traveling, and drinking coffee.

www.ingramcontent.com/pod-product-compliance
Lightning Source LLC
LaVergne TN
LVHW041524070426
835507LV00012B/1800